STRENGTH IN PRAYER

TEACH ME
GOD'S WORD SERIES

C. P. SUMMERFIELD

AuthorHouse™ UK
1663 Liberty Drive
Bloomington, IN 47403 USA
www.authorhouse.co.uk
UK TFN: 0800 0148641 (Toll Free inside the UK)
UK Local: 02036 956322 (+44 20 3695 6322 from outside the UK)

Bible Scripture: King James Version

This book is printed on acid-free paper.

ISBN: 979-8-8230-9129-9 (sc)
ISBN: 979-8-8230-9130-5 (e)

Library of Congress Control Number: 2024927169

Print information available on the last page.

Published by AuthorHouse   01/09/2025

authorHOUSE®

CONTENTS

AUTHOR'S NOTE

As you read this book you will come to understand some important lessons from the Bible. We focus on how to pray and how to get answers from God. Above all this book aims to help you learn and love the Bible.

This book focuses on Biblical records that teach principles for life and how to trust God. In turn, these principles build a strong character, build confidence, teach courage and show you how to stand tall in any situation. You'll also see that these are the characteristics and life skills that God wants for you. God wants us to be strong and successful in life.

God created humanity so that He would have a family; God as our Father and we as His children. You will see how God consistently takes care of His family and at the same time has given people freedom to choose. He never forces anyone to believe Him or to love Him.

God has given us His Word in the Bible so that we can know Him. Life offers up lots of distractions, but it is God's Word that has the answers for any situation. You will learn that it is as relevant and dynamic today as it was in biblical times.

You will find that there are direct quotes from the Bible in this book. This is done so that you can see for yourself what the Bible says (that's especially important), you can go into your own Bible and find the quote yourself and in the process, you can become familiar and come to love it. This book uses the King James Version; you may find the old English strange at first, but it'll grow on you soon enough.

The Bible is an ancient collection of books that were written over the course of thousands of years. During that time, how God worked with people changed. For example, the children of Israel lived under the law that God had given to Moses, but we are no longer under the law because the law was fulfilled with the work of Jesus Christ. We live after the time of Jesus Christ and enjoy the wonderful blessings that his accomplished work made available.

There are records in this book from the Old Testament including the times before the law, during the time of the law, and then records from the time of Christ and the New Testament. Collectively these records teach valuable lessons about prayer, believing God and His Word. Later books in the Series will build on these lessons and continue to unfold the Word of God.

I hope that you enjoy reading this book and it helps you grow your knowledge of the Word of God.

INTRODUCTION

The series Teach Me God's Word aims to open up the Biblical scriptures for young inquisitive minds. The records within the Bible come alive as we understand the principles of biblical research. In this book we focus on what the Word says about prayer, how to pray and about what is available. Once we understand these simple truths, we can build an effective prayer life and have a conversation with God so that we can enjoy the bountiful life of prayer. Peoples' knowledge and trust in God have built character and strength in humanity throughout the ages and continues to do so today.

There is a scripture in the book of Psalms that shows us that God wants to hear from us. He wants us to talk to Him.

> Psalms 62:8Trust in him at all times; ye people, pour out your heart before him: God *is* a refuge for us. Selah.

God encourages us to pour out our hearts to Him, that is completely unloading the things that you care about or the things that burden you to God. God is a refuge, a safe place for us, He will protect. He is a refuge.

Let's focus our attention on prayer, what is it to pray? How do we pray? What is it that we pray for? What do we do while we wait for answers to our prayers? These questions will be answered in this book so that you can learn all about prayer and to build your unique relationship with God, our heavenly Father.

CONFIDENCE

I John 5:14-15 And this is the confidence that we have in him, that, if we ask any thing according to his will, he heareth us: And if we know that he hear us, whatsoever we ask, we know that we have the petitions that we desired of him.

God hears you when you ask any thing according to his will. Well, how do you know God's will? His will is contained in His Word! You can have confidence that God hears your prayer.

We will explore some of the things God wants for our lives. Things like good health, our needs supplied, prosperity, and an abundant life. These are things we should have that are according to God's will; we can pray for these things in our lives and the lives of our loved ones.

Proverbs 15:8b ...but the prayer of the upright is his delight.

God delights in your prayers! He is delighted to hear from you.

Let's look some more at what the Word says about prayer!

JESUS TEACHES PRAYER

Let's start with a record in the gospels where Jesus Christ teaches people how to pray. What we should do and, just as importantly, what not to do!

> Matthew 6: 1-2 Take heed that ye do not your alms before men, to be seen of them: otherwise ye have no reward of your Father which is in heaven. Therefore when thou doest *thine alms, do not sound a trumpet before thee, as the hypocrites do in the synagogues and in the streets, that they may have glory of men. Verily I say unto you, They have their reward.*

Firstly, Jesus opens the chapter about prayer by first discussing the giving of alms. Alms refers to the requirement under the Mosiac law to give charitably, to support others. Jesus teaches this is not something that should be done to look good, "look at me, I am so righteous and religious." That must have been very commonplace in the synagogues at the time when some people wanted others to see how godly they were. They were seeking the glory or praise of other people and that was their reward, to be seen and admired by them. This does not qualify for God's admiration. God respects giving from the heart.

> 3-6 But when thou doest alms, let not thy left hand know what thy right hand doeth: That thine alms may be in secret: and thy Father which seeth in secret himself shall reward thee openly. And when thou prayest, thou shalt not be as the hypocrites are: for they love to pray standing in the synagogues and in the corners of the streets, that they may be seen of men. Verily I say unto you, They have their reward. But thou, when thou prayest, enter into thy closet, and when thou hast shut thy door, pray to thy Father which is in secret; and thy Father which seeth in secret shall reward thee openly.

With that comparison, Jesus teaches that when you pray it should be private between you and God, a private relationship. Imagine praying in your closet where only God sees or hears you, although this does not mean literally. God wants you to talk to Him, quietly, privately, it's your conversation with God. But look at how you will be rewarded? Openly for all to see.

5

7-8 But when ye pray, use not vain repetitions, as the heathen do: for they think that they shall be heard for their much speaking. Be not ye therefore like unto them: for your Father knoweth what things ye have need of, before ye ask him.

Next thing that Jesus addresses is the structure of the prayer. We are not to use meaningless repetition. In the lands and times of the Bible the other nations were called 'heathens' or sometimes 'gentiles' and they would pray by chanting, were they repeat the same words over and over. Very clearly Jesus teaches us not to do this, instead he gives an example of a prayer.

9-13 After this manner therefore pray ye: Our Father which art in heaven, Hallowed be thy name. Thy kingdom come. Thy will be done in earth, as it is in heaven. Give us this day our daily bread. And forgive us our debts, as we forgive our debtors. And lead us not into temptation, but deliver us from evil: For thine is the kingdom, and the power, and the glory, for ever. Amen.

This is the very famous prayer 'Our Father', which Jesus gives as an example of prayer. In this example, he starts by praising God his heavenly Father and prays for His Kingdom that was to come. (Jesus Christ brought about the Kingdom by the work he accomplished, however at the time of speaking Jesus still looked forward to that Kingdom). He prayed that God's will would be done here on Earth, and he asks God to supply his needs, for his food and nourishment. He asks in the prayer for forgiveness for wrongs or failings and prays that we forgive those who fail or wrong us. He then requests that God direct his path away from temptation and evil and then finishes as it started, praising God, His power and glory.

What a wonderful prayer! We give thanks to God and praise Him. We ask him to supply our needs, we ask Him to direct our path and protect us from evil. We can ask him to forgive us when we fail and pray for the strength to forgive others. Then we can praise God again, He is all powerful, willing, and able!

God encourages prayer, he wants us to talk to him privately and He will answer, He will protect and He will supply.

DON'T EAT THE STEAK

Let's now jump back in time to when Israel and Judah had been captured by the King of Babylon and let's take a look at how God answered the prayers of a few courageous young men.

This record in Daniel will show the results of men who prayed in a life and death situation and God answered their prayers. Let's get some background on the situation at the time.

> 11Kings24:11 And Nebuchadnezzar king of Babylon came against the city, and his servants did besiege it.

Nebuchadnezzar was the great King of Babylon, he was a powerful King. Nebuchadnezzar ruled a great empire; the Babylonian Empire. This empire consisted of a huge region from Syria to Egypt, and from Iraq to Israel. Nebuchadnezzar and his army had conquered all the nations in between and they had taken captive Israel and Judah. His armies stole all the treasures from the house of God and took their skilled men and women as slaves. The children of Israel had walked away from God and as a result they walked away from God's protection which opened the door to persecution and captivity.

> 13-14 And he carried out thence all the treasures of the house of the Lord, and the treasures of the king's house, and cut in pieces all the vessels of gold which Solomon king of Israel had made in the temple of the Lord, as the Lord had said. And he carried away all Jerusalem, and all the princes, and all the mighty men of valour, even ten thousand captives, and all the craftsmen and smiths: none remained, save the poorest sort of the people of the land.

Nebuchadnezzar took only the brightest people, the best military men, the best craftsmen, the most talented people back to Babylon. He then ordered that the best of the best would be groomed to serve him in his palace.

Daniel 1:4 Children in whom was no blemish, but well favoured, and skilful in all wisdom, and cunning in knowledge, and understanding science, and such as had ability in them to stand in the king's palace, and whom they might teach the learning and the tongue of the Chaldeans.

The King wanted to ensure that the selected captives were well fed with food fit for a king, food from his table, so that they could be at their best to serve in his kingdom.

5-6 And the king appointed them a daily provision of the king's meat, and of the wine which he drank: so nourishing them three years, that at the end thereof they might stand before the king.

Now among these were of the children of Judah; Daniel, Hananiah, Mishael, and Azariah: Four young captives; Daniel, Hananiah, Mishael and Azariah were chosen to take part in the King's training program.

8 But Daniel purposed in his heart that he would not defile himself with the portion of the king's meat, nor with the wine which he drank: therefore, he requested of the prince of the eunuchs that he might not defile himself.

Daniel did not want to eat the food from the King's table! There was something that bothered Daniel, he knew that food from the Kings table would be dedicated to false Gods. Daniel loved God and did not want to eat food dedicated to any other god. He was not afraid to reject the offer of the very best food even though he was already a captive and not really in a bargaining position. Daniel was not going to back down; he asked the prince in charge if he could eat something else.

9-10 Now God had brought Daniel into favour and tender love with the prince of the eunuchs. And the prince of the eunuchs said unto Daniel, I fear my lord the king, who hath appointed your meat and your drink: for why should he see your faces worse liking than the children which are of your sort? then shall ye make me endanger my head to the king.

The prince in charge had grown to respect Daniel, Daniel had obviously proven himself to be an honorable person. So, the prince considered his request, but he had a major concern and that was the safety of his head! He liked it attached to his neck. He argued that if he did not give Daniel and his friends the best food that the King would notice that they did not look as well as the other captives and the King would have his head! But Daniel had a proposition.

> 12 Prove thy servants, I beseech thee, ten days; and let them give us pulse to eat, and water to drink.

Daniel proposed that for 10 days he and his three friends would eat only beans, lentils and water and then they could be compared to the others, then the prince could decide. At the end of the ten-day test Daniel and his three friends looked much healthier than those captives who ate from the King's table.

> 17 As for these four children, God gave them knowledge and skill in all learning and wisdom: and Daniel had understanding in all visions and dreams.

These brave young men stood up for what they believed in and were not afraid. Not that they were vegetarians but rather they would not eat food dedicated to the gods of Babylon. When they stood for God, he blessed their lives, they grew in knowledge and wisdom. Daniel himself developed a special understanding to interpret visions and dreams.

> 18-20 Now at the end of the days that the king had said he should bring them in, then the prince of the eunuchs brought them in before Nebuchadnezzar. And the king communed with them; and among them all was found none like Daniel, Hananiah, Mishael, and Azariah: therefore, stood they before the King. And in all matters of wisdom and understanding, that the King enquired of them, he found them ten times better than all the magicians and astrologers that were in all his realm.

These four young men took a stand for God without fear of the consequences, they were slaves in Babylon, the centre of the empire and they were not in a position to be making special requests.

But they trusted God would protect them if they stood on His Word. They refused to eat foods dedicated to other Gods; God did not let them down. As God worked with them, they grew in wisdom and knowledge so much so that when they were finally presented to the King, they were ten times better than all of the King's men.

Up until this point we can see the faithfulness and respect that these young men had for God. So, with this background let's look at the next book of Daniel.

13

WHAT DREAM?

Daniel 2:1-3 And in the second year of the reign of Nebuchadnezzar, Nebuchadnezzar dreamed dreams, wherewith his spirit was troubled, and his sleep brake from him. Then the king commanded to call the magicians, and the astrologers, and the sorcerers, and the Chaldeans, for to shew the king his dreams. So they came and stood before the king. And the king said unto them, I have dreamed a dream, and my spirit was troubled to know the dream.

King Nebuchadnezzar had a dream, and it troubled him so much that he could not sleep. He ordered his counselors to tell him what the dream meant. They asked him to tell them the dream.

5 The king answered and said to the Chaldeans, The thing is gone from me: if ye will not make known unto me the dream, with the interpretation thereof, ye shall be cut in pieces, and your houses shall be made a dunghill.

The problem was King Nebuchadnezzar could not remember the dream! So, as he was the King he could make up his own rules. But, in a kingly fashion he threatened his counselors that if they could not tell him the dream and the interpretation of the dream, he was going to have them killed and destroy everything they owned. This King was a fearful tyrant.

6 But if ye shew the dream, and the interpretation thereof, ye shall receive of me gifts and rewards and great honour: therefore shew me the dream, and the interpretation thereof.

On the other hand, if the counselors told him the dream and the meaning of the dream, he would reward him richly. Which was great news if any of them knew the dream and the interpretation. Regrettably, his counselors did not and understandably disputed with the King that what he asked was impossible. No one could do such a thing, or could they?

10-12 The Chaldeans answered before the king, and said, There is not a man upon the earth that can shew the king's matter: therefore there is no king, lord, nor ruler, that asked such things at any magician, or astrologer, or Chaldean. And it is a rare thing that the king requireth, and there is none other that can shew it before the king, except the gods, whose dwelling is not with flesh. For this cause the king was angry and very furious, and commanded to destroy all the wise men of Babylon.

That did not please the King, he was pretty mad with his counsel and commanded that all the wise men that serve him should be killed.

13-15 And the decree went forth that the wise men should be slain; and they sought Daniel and his fellows to be slain. Then Daniel answered with counsel and wisdom to Arioch the captain of the king's guard, which was gone forth to slay the wise men of Babylon: He answered and said to Arioch the king's captain, Why is the decree so hasty from the king? Then Arioch made the thing known to Daniel.

Daniel when he found out that his life was in danger wondered why the King was in such a hurry? Daniel needed some time. What was Daniel to do? Well, he immediately looked to God to solve the problem.

16-18 Then Daniel went in, and desired of the king that he would give him time, and that he would shew the king the interpretation. Then Daniel went to his house, and made the thing known to Hananiah, Mishael, and Azariah, his companions: That they would desire mercies of the God of heaven concerning this secret; that Daniel and his fellows should not perish with the rest of the wise men of Babylon.

Daniel explained the dangerous position they were in to his three friends; Hanaiah, Mishael and Azariah and what did they do? They prayed and asked God to save them.

19-20 Then was the secret revealed unto Daniel in a night vision. Then Daniel blessed the God of heaven. Daniel answered and said, Blessed be the name of God for ever and ever: for wisdom and might are his:

God did not let them down; He revealed the dream and its interpretation to Daniel. Daniel was so thankful that he prayed a beautiful prayer thanking God for His power, His grace, and His wisdom. Daniel and his three friends had prayed to God when their lives were in danger; they trusted God to give them the answer. God never fails us when we believe.

24-25 Therefore Daniel went in unto Arioch, whom the king had ordained to destroy the wise men of Babylon: he went and said thus unto him; Destroy not the wise men of Babylon: bring me in before the king, and I will shew unto the king the interpretation. Then Arioch brought in Daniel before the king in haste, and said thus unto him, I have found a man of the captives of Judah, that will make known unto the king the interpretation.

Daniel has a chat with Arioch, the man who was commissioned to carry out the King's order to destroy all the wise men. Daniel wanted to speak to the King and give him the interpretation of the dream. Arioch rushed Daniel in before King Nebuchadnezzar.

The King spoke to Daniel and asked him if he could remember the dream and give the interpretation. Daniel gave a beautiful response; he gave the glory to God.

28 But there is a God in heaven that revealeth secrets, and maketh known to the king Nebuchadnezzar what shall be in the latter days.

Daniel bravely told the King what his dream was and what it meant. The King was overwhelmed.

46-48Then the king Nebuchadnezzar fell upon his face, and worshipped Daniel, and commanded that they should offer an oblation and sweet odours unto him. The king answered unto Daniel, and said, Of a truth it is, that your God is a God of gods, and a Lord of kings, and a revealer of secrets, seeing thou couldest reveal this secret. Then the king made Daniel a great man, and gave him many great gifts, and made him ruler over the whole province of Babylon, and chief of the governors over all the wise men of Babylon.

Look at what King Nebuchadnezzar said about God, a 'God of gods' and 'Lord of Kings'. The King then made Daniel ruler over the whole province. But Daniel wanted to take care of his friends and made a petition to the King on behalf of them.

49 Then Daniel requested of the king, and he set Shadrach, Meshach, and Abednego, over the affairs of the province of Babylon: but Daniel sat in the gate of the king.

Daniel's friends, Hananiah, Mishael, and Azariah had been given new names in Babylon; Shadrach, Meshach, and Abednego. They prayed for an answer from God when their lives were in danger. God answered giving Daniel the detail and meaning of the King's dream. They trusted God and not only did they eliminate the threat to their lives, but Daniel and his friends became the rulers over the affairs of Babylon. What a journey from captives to rulers!

YOU ARE BETTER

Matthew 6:25-26 Therefore I say unto you, Take no thought for your life, what ye shall eat, or what ye shall drink; nor yet for your body, what ye shall put on. Is not the life more than meat, and the body than raiment? Behold the fowls of the air: for they sow not, neither do they reap, nor gather into barns; yet your heavenly Father feedeth them. Are ye not much better than they?

In the book of Matthew Jesus teaches it is better to believe God rather than choosing to worry. Worry and fear are the opposite of believing.

We all need to eat; drink and put some clothes on but these things should never cause us to worry. Birds do not need to sow, nor harvest, not gather their food into stores and yet God takes care of them. Jesus asks, are you not better than birds? The answer is, of course, yes, yes we are!

27 Which of you by taking thought can add one cubit unto his stature?

Jesus asks, 'can you think yourself into being taller?' The answer is, of course, no! So why put so much thought into our wardrobe?

28-30 And why take ye thought for raiment? Consider the lilies of the field, how they grow; they toil not, neither do they spin: And yet I say unto you, That even Solomon in all his glory was not arrayed like one of these. Wherefore, if God so clothe the grass of the field, which today is, and tomorrow is cast into the oven, shall he not much more clothe you, O ye of little faith?

Have you ever seen a lily of the field? They are very beautiful flowers, and they just grow. God created them to do just that. Solomon who was one of the riches Kings ever to reign over Israel, dressed in the finest robes and yet they never came close to the beauty of the lilies. If God takes care of them, shall he not do more for you? The answer is, of course, yes!

33-34 But seek ye first the kingdom of God, and his righteousness; and all these things shall be added unto you. Take therefore no thought for the morrow: for the morrow shall take thought for the things of itself. Sufficient unto the day is the evil thereof.

Jesus teaches to seek God first and He will supply. We have no need to worry about today or tomorrow, God will still be God tomorrow. He will still answer our prayers, and He will supply our needs.

BE ANXIOUS FOR NOTHING

Philippians 4:6 Be careful for nothing; but in everything by prayer and supplication with thanksgiving let your requests be made known unto God.

The word 'careful' is better understood as 'anxious'. Here we are told again to be anxious for nothing! Instead, in everything pray, and let God know what you need. Pray with thanksgiving because it is important to remember all that God does for you.

So now we have a tool to combat anxieties. Pray! When you start to find yourself worrying or getting stressed take a step back and pray.

Philippians 4:19 But my God shall supply all your need according to his riches in glory by Christ Jesus.

God supplies our need, don't stress, instead pray.

Do you know how God wants you to live? Very well! He has got you covered!

PROSPERTY AND HEALTH

This next record reveals a lot about how loving and caring God is.

>III John 2 Beloved, I wish above all things that thou mayest prosper and be in health, even as thy soul prospereth.

How does your soul prosper? As you continue to believe God's Word you prosper and are healthy. If this is what the Word declares then these are things that are available, and we can pray for them.

So, let's break that down a little; if God wants us to prosper and be in health as our soul prospers then He certainly does not want us to be poor nor lacking.

If God wants us to be in health, then He certainly does not want us to be ill nor would He put things in our way that would cause us illness. That would not be God's design, things that make us ill are not from God.

If God wants us to prosper and be in health as our soul prospers then He certainly does want us to know Him. How does our soul prosper? By learning His Word and living the Word He has given us.

ABUNDANCE

Have you ever been to a food festival where there is such an abundance of food you do not know what to choose? Or think about the table at Christmas or Thanksgiving where there is an abundance of food. Look at what Jesus says about abundance.

> John 10:10 The thief cometh not, but for to steal, and to kill, and to destroy: I am come that they might have life, and that they might have it more abundantly.

Jesus was on a mission; he came for the specific purpose to give life and a life that is more abundant. Whatever life came before him was not enough. He had come so that people might have something new; a life and to have it more abundantly.

There is a Thief on the other hand that only comes to kill, steal and destroy. But not Jesus Christ. So, we want to ensure that we benefit from what Jesus made available and that we do not get tricked by the Thief. An abundant life sounds really good, don't you think? To live a more abundant life is God's desire for our lives.

PRAY & BELIEVE

Mark 11:24 Therefore I say unto you, What things soever ye desire, when ye pray, believe that ye receive them, and ye shall have them.

Jesus Christ teaches his disciples, in this verse in Mark, about prayer. Once we know what God has made available to us in His Word or by revelation we can pray, and when we pray, we believe God's Word. To receive anything from God, we must believe what God has said in His Word.

God is able, He is willing, look at what He tells us about Himself in these scriptures.

Matthew 21:22 And all things, whatsoever ye shall ask in prayer, believing, ye shall receive.

Once we know what God has made available to us, we pray, and we believe His Word.

John 14:13 – 14 And whatsoever ye shall ask in my name, that will I do, that the Father may be glorified in the Son. If ye shall ask any thing in my name, I will do it.

Jesus Christ specifically tells us here in the gospel of John that we can ask things of God in the name of Jesus Christ. He says that when we ask anything in his name, he will do it.

Remember we already know that we can pray for things according to God's will. The Word of God will never contradict itself, so when we pray in Jesus Christ's name according to the Word, Jesus Christ says he will do it!

THE UNJUST JUDGE

Jesus taught a lot about prayer and in this next record Jesus teaches that we should not give up in our prayers.

> Luke 18:1 And he spake a parable unto them to this end, that men ought always to pray, and not to faint.

A parable is like a picture story that teaches one special point. There may be many elements to the story but there is one main point that makes up the focus of the story. Jesus often taught in parables and they are not always easily understood. Thankfully with this parable, Jesus makes very clear from the start his purpose in teaching it. 'that people should always pray and not faint'; they should not give up. When they pray they should persevere, remaining consistent and continuing in prayer.

> 2 Saying, there was in a city a judge, which feared not God, neither regarded man:

The Judge in this parable was neither nice nor particularly good. At this time in Israel, Rome governed the region, and many judges were put in place to uphold Roman rule.

> 3-5 And there was a widow in that city; and she came unto him, saying, Avenge me of mine adversary. And he would not for a while: but afterward he said within himself, Though I fear not God, nor regard man; Yet because this widow troubleth me, I will avenge her, lest by her continual coming she weary me.

A widow presented herself to the judge seeking justice against her adversary. We do not know what her case was about nor do we know who her adversary was, but we do know that the widow was persistent. This widow would not give up, she pleaded with the Judge until eventually the Judge grew so tired of her that he agreed to help. In the hope she would leave him alone!

6-8 And the Lord said, Hear what the unjust judge saith. And shall not God avenge his own elect, which cry day and night unto him, though he bear long with them? I tell you that he will avenge them speedily.

Remember there is one main point to a parable and in this one we are told from the start that the point is that 'men ought always to pray and not to faint'. The comparison is that we are to pray like the widow, we are to be consistent, we are to persevere, we do not give up.

God is not likened to the selfish Judge. In fact, He answers with speed. We know that God delights in our prayers, He supplies our needs, He hears us when we pray, He wants us to pour out our hearts to Him! The point being taught is that WE pray, and WE persevere just like that very determined widow.

EFFECTUAL PRAYERS

James 5:16b-18 The effectual fervent prayer of a righteous man availeth much. Elias was a man subject to like passions as we are, and he prayed earnestly that it might not rain: and it rained not on the earth by the space of three years and six months. And he prayed again, and the heaven gave rain, and the earth brought forth her fruit.

Prayer is 'effectual' that means effective; Prayer is very effective.

There was a man of God called Elijah, and he prayed that it would not rain for three years, and six months and it didn't. You can read this in I Kings 17 – 19.

A man that stood for God when all around him did not. When he prayed God answered and that is why prayers are effectual! God answers our prayers, He answered Elijah, He answered Daniel and friends and He will answer your prayers.

PRAY WITHOUT CEASING

There is a record in the book of Acts that shows the effective results of prayer and continuing in prayer. The disciples were out teaching the Word in the first century church and the rulers did not like it. They disliked it so much that Herod the King ordered an assault against the Christians.

Acts 12:1-3 Now about that time Herod the King stretched forth his hands to vex certain of the church. And he killed James the brother of John with the sword. And because he saw it pleased the Jews, he proceeded further to take Peter also. (Then were the days of unleavened bread.)

This was a very dangerous time to be a Christian. James, one of Jesus Christ's disciples, had been killed and Peter was arrested.

4-5 And when he had apprehended him, he put him in prison, and delivered him to four quaternions of soldiers to keep him; intending after Easter to bring him forth to the people. Peter therefore was kept in prison: but prayer was made without ceasing of the church unto God for him.

All the while Peter was in prison the believers continued without ceasing to pray for Peter.

6-9 And when Herod would have brought him forth, the same night Peter was sleeping between two soldiers, bound with two chains: and the keepers before the door kept the prison. And, behold, the angel of the Lord came upon him, and a light shined in the prison: and he smote Peter on the side, and raised him up, saying, Arise up quickly. And his chains fell off from his hands. And the angel said unto him, Gird thyself, and bind on thy sandals. And so he did. And he saith unto him, Cast thy garment about thee, and follow me. And he went out, and followed him; and wist not that it was true which was done by the angel; but thought he saw a vision.

During the night an angel came to Peter who was chained between two soldiers. The angel wakes Peter up by poking his side and tells him to arise. The chains fall from Peter's hands and the angel instructs him to get ready to leave, put on his coat, his sandals and follow him. Peter followed but he was in a haze thinking that this whole experience was not real but only a vision. Was he dreaming?

> 10-11 When they were past the first and the second ward, they came unto the iron gate that leadeth unto the city; which opened to them of his own accord: and they went out, and passed on through one street; and forthwith the angel departed from him. And when Peter was come to himself, he said, Now I know of a surety, that the Lord hath sent his angel, and hath delivered me out of the hand of Herod, and from all the expectation of the people of the Jews.

Once Peter was safely freed from the prison, the angel left him and it was only then that he realized what just happened, it was real, it was not a vision.

> 12And when he had considered the thing, he came to the house of Mary the mother of John, whose surname was Mark; where many were gathered together praying. And as Peter knocked at the door of the gate, a damsel came to hearken, named Rhoda. And when she knew Peter's voice, she opened not the gate for gladness, but ran in, and told how Peter stood before the gate.

Peter hurried to his friend's house where many of the believers were praying for him. He knocked on the door and waited. Rhoda a young girl came to answer the door and when she heard Peter's voice rather than let Peter in she runs back inside to tell everyone that Peter is at the door!

> 15And they said unto her, Thou art mad. But she constantly affirmed that it was even so. Then said they, It is his angel.

This was hard to believe! How could Peter be at the door, he was arrested earlier and was in prison? It must be an angel they thought.

16But Peter continued knocking: and when they had opened the door, and saw him, they were astonished.

Meanwhile Peter still outside the gate kept knocking! When they finally opened the door they were astonished. Peter was at the door. How could this be?

When people get together to pray wonderful things happen. When people continue in prayer they see results just like Peter and his friends.

PRAY TOGETHER

Matthew 18: 19-20 Again I say unto you, That if two of you shall agree on earth as touching any thing that they shall ask, it shall be done for them of my Father which is in heaven. For where two or three are gathered together in my name, there am I in the midst of them.

Jesus Christ teaches in these beautiful little verses, that when you pray together with others, the prayer will be answered. In fact, when we get together to pray, we are not alone.

We have already read, that God hears us, that Jesus Christ is in the midst when we pray together, that when we pray according to God's will, we can expect results.

Critical common denominator is that we believe God and what His Word says. Not doubt, not worry, but an unwavering belief that God supplies!

What a blessing to be able to pray together with our loved ones and to pray for each other.

ABOUT THE AUTHOR

Clare Summerfield grew up a Christian and has spent many decades searching out the truths of God's Word. She has taken numerous Biblical Research courses over this time and read extensively on the subject.

Clare is the mother of three adult children and has brought them up to know God and to trust Him and His Word. Teaching the Word of God to children builds trust in God, a confidence and strength of character.

She is committed to devoting her energy to teaching the Word of God to children in a simple and succinct way. This series of 'Teach me God's Word' is dedicated to her children and their children.

> Proverbs 22:6 Train up a child in the way he should go: and when he is old, he will not depart from it.

ACKNOWLEDGEMENTS

I thank my heavenly Father for His love and care. For the Word that He has given us so that we can know Him.

I thank my Lord and Saviour Jesus Christ for his accomplished work of redemption.

> John 3:16 -17 For God so loved the world, that he gave his only begotten Son, that whosoever believeth in him should not perish, but have everlasting life. For God sent not his Son into the world to condemn the world; but that the world through him might be saved.

It amazes me how through the centuries the Bible has been protected so that we have it available today. What a privilege it is to know the Word and to have the freedom to speak it.

I thank Rebecca for her valuable insight and help with the presentation of his book. I thank the numerous contributors to this work and the people in my life that have helped me come to understand God's Word. They know who they are. There is so much more to go, and I look forward to it.

What a joy to live in a day and time that we can know our Father and His wonderful son Jesus Christ.

BIBLIOGRAPHY

Version, K. J. (1990). Companion Bible. Grand Rapids Michigan: Kregel Publications.

Bible, Kings James Version...

Printed in the United States
by Baker & Taylor Publisher Services